Collins

Revised Edition

Vision 4

A Course on Values and Life Skills

Main menu
Learning objects
Search book or online
Page jump
Mark-up data
View fullscreen
Help menu
Bookmark page
Open tool panel
Insert note
Pen & highlight
Single/double page
Zoom in
Zoom out
Zoom 100%
Sound on/off
Record audio
Spotlight
Clear data
Interactive whiteboard mode
Collins DIGISUITE
Search here
Online Search
Page 14-15 / 24
All Pages
Table of Contents
Animation
Audio
Interactivities
Teacher's Resource
Learning Tools
Test Generator
Dictionary
IWB
READING
Read this poem and see what a sister does to take care of her little brother.
Little, helpless baby dear,
While within your cot you lie,
Sister is sitting near
She will sing your lullaby.
When at last you fall asleep,
Not the slightest noise she'll make;
Quiet as a mouse she'll keep,
Without letting her darling wake.
helpless: unable to take care of yourself
cot: a small bed with high sides for a baby
lullaby: a soft gentle song sung to make a child go to sleep
slightest: very small
quiet: making no noise
darling: a person who is loved very much by somebody
wake: to stop sleeping
26
COMPREHENSION
A. Choose the correct option.
1. The baby's sister is sitting
a. near the baby.
b. far from the baby.
c. in another room.
2. The baby's sister will
a. sing a lullaby.
b. play with the baby.
c. wake up the baby.
B. Answer the questions.
1. Where is the baby lying?
2. Who will keep quiet like a mouse?
3. How is the baby's sister? Think of and write two words to describe her.
Life Skills and Values
Caring for one's family
1. Imagine you are playing outside your house, and your little brother is sleeping inside alone. Suddenly you hear your brother cry. What would you do?
2. You are watching TV with your friend. Your sister is sleeping in the next room. Your friend asks you to raise the volume of the TV. What would you do?
27

Preface

Vision Revised Edition, a course on life skills and values, is an engaging value education series meant to enable learners lead a balanced, happy and successful life. The National Education Policy, 2020 proposes the revision and revamping of all aspects of the education structure to create a new system that is aligned with the aspirational goals of 21st century education, while building upon India's traditions and value systems. It also lays focus on critical life skills and values.

Vision Revised Edition follows an interactive and multidisciplinary approach and caters to all kinds of learners with different learning styles.

Values are presented through progressively graded stories, anecdotes or poems.

Life Skills as laid down by the World Health Organization (WHO) have been covered through interesting stories.

Each book contains special chapters and colourful spreads showcasing the **United Nations Sustainable Development Goals**, which are important to achieve a just and an equitable world for all.

21st Century Skills have been mapped to each chapter with the aim of creating well-rounded individuals thriving in a constantly changing world.

Mental health and well-being of young learners is of prime importance in today's world. Therefore, **Let's Do Yoga** poster has been introduced as a brand-new feature of the book. It contains simple and doable asanas with step-by-step guidance and illustrations.

The series also focuses on mindfulness and social-emotional learning through **'happiness activities'**. Young children learn by doing, hence the series has a variety of hands-on activities, encouraging quiet reflection and sound action.

Creating a safety net for children and making them aware of **child rights** is much needed in this age and time. *Vision* Revised Edition has special advice for children through which they can face situations in which they feel afraid, pressurized or unsafe.

Vision Revised Edition comes with **Collins DigiSuite** which offers digital content packed with animated stories, slideshows and interactive activities.

***Vision* Teacher's Manuals** offer comprehensive **Lesson Plans** and **Additional Worksheets** for teachers.

In This Series ...

Vision Revised Edition adheres to the National Education Policy, 2020. Features such as 21st Century Skills, Life Skills, multiple intelligences, Sustainable Development Goals and Let's Do Yoga all align with the new policy.

Discuss

Warm-up exercise familiarizes students to the mood of the chapter

Read along

A story or a poem based on a value

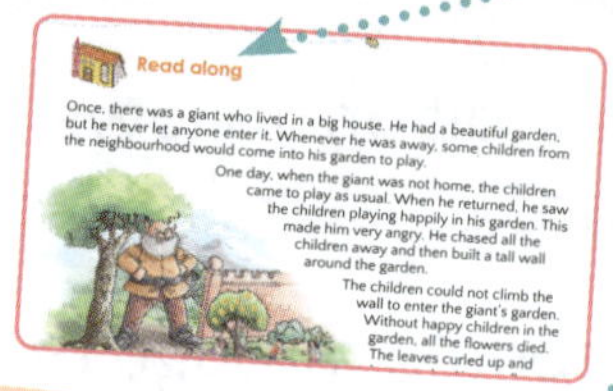

Figure out

Questions based on the chapter to ensure value inculcation

Figure out

Tick (✓) the correct answers.

1. The giant made a high wall around the garden because
   a. he did not want the children to play in his garden.
   b. he loved the children.

Project

Interesting projects based on the values taught

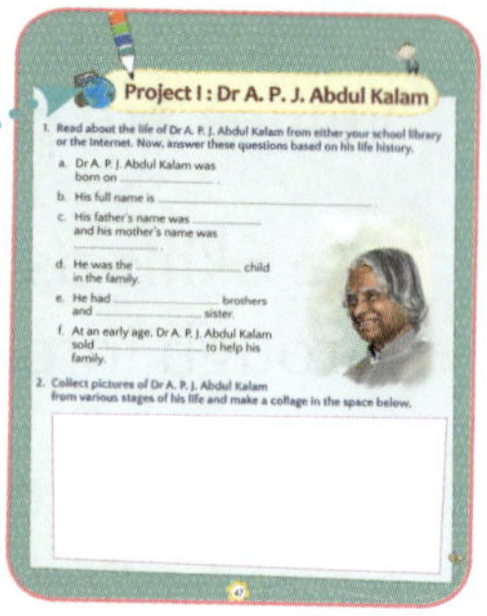

Relate

Application-based questions to check students' understanding

Relate

Draw a 🙂 for the best answer.

1. Your father made pasta for you. You know that your friend loves pasta. What would you do?
   a. I would pack some pasta for my friend.
   b. I would eat the pasta all by myself.

Happiness Activity

Interesting activities to promote 'happiness'

Workout

Interesting worksheets that reinforce the value taught

Remember

Brief pointers that the students can incorporate in their behaviour

Remember

- Share your thoughts and feelings with your parents.
- Share your toys and games with your friends and cousins.
- Share your notes with your classmates.
- Take care of things that are shared with you.
- Remember, sharing is a good habit.

Think and Say

Thinking questions that encourage students to think laterally

Think and Say

When you come home wet on a rainy day, what do your parents do? Do you like that?

Happiness Box

Enjoyable activities that promote 'happiness' and exercises based on multiple intelligences addressing different learning styles

- Musical
- Interpersonal
- Visual-Spatial
- Verbal linguistic
- Naturalistic
- Intrapersonal
- Logical Mathematical
- Bodily Kinesthetic

Child Rights and Empowerment

Useful, child-centric advice to create a safety net for children and make them aware of their rights

Sustainable Development Goals

Special chapter and a colourful spread showcasing the UN Sustainable Development Goals, a set of goals aimed at changing our world for better

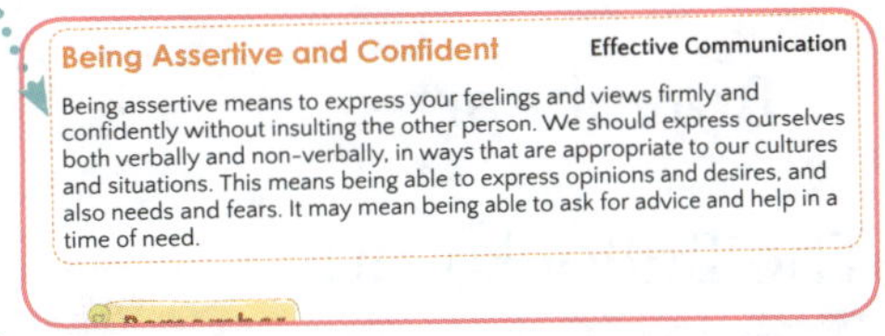
Being Assertive and Confident — Effective Communication

Being assertive means to express your feelings and views firmly and confidently without insulting the other person. We should express ourselves both verbally and non-verbally, in ways that are appropriate to our cultures and situations. This means being able to express opinions and desires, and also needs and fears. It may mean being able to ask for advice and help in a time of need.

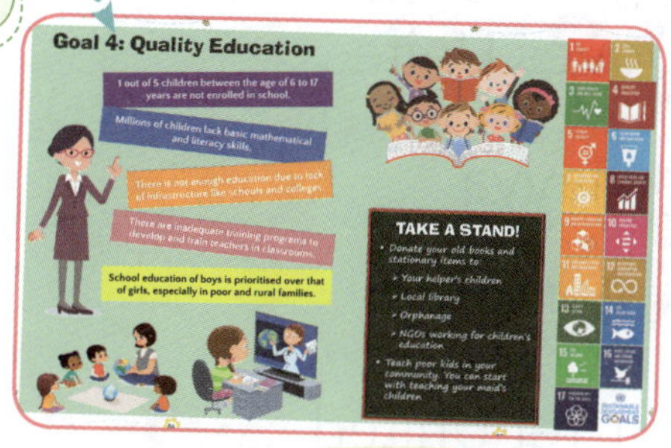

Poster

Colourful and interesting pull-out poster showcasing easy Yoga asanas

21st Century Skills

Skills necessary to succeed in the age of information: learning skills, literacy skills and social skills

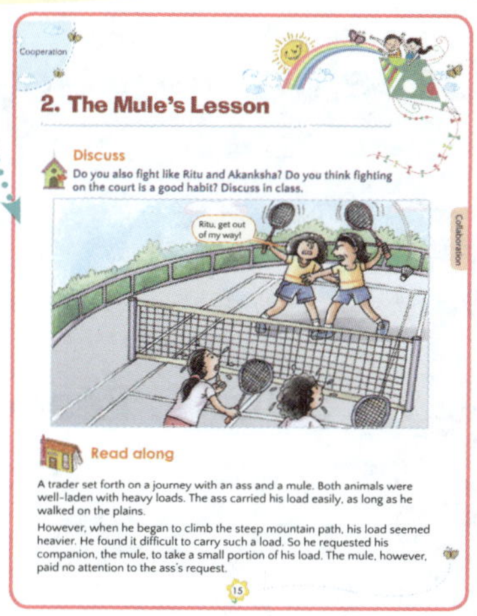

Life Skills

Chapters focusing on WHO life skills through interesting stories

Teaching tips

- Talk about how strong determination helps the boy cross the stream.
- Tell children more stories about determination.

Teaching tips

Suggestions for teachers

Detailed Contents

Sustainable Development Goals

21st Century Skills

Learning Skills	Collaboration	The Mule's Lesson The Bullock Cart
	Communication	The Humble Scholar
	Critical Thinking	The Doves Unite
Literacy Skills	Cultural and Civic Literacy	Different Yet United
Social Skills	Flexibility	The Angry Giant
	Initiative	Braveheart
	Persistence	Ekalavya
	Citizenship	Qutub Minar

Life Skills

Tina Goes Camping Sid Wants a Robot	Critical Thinking Self-awareness

Projects

Project I Project II	Dr A. P. J. Abdul Kalam Unity in Diversity

Contents

1. The Angry Giant

Discuss

Sharing things with our siblings is so much fun. Do you share things with your siblings? Discuss in class.

Read along

Once, there was a giant who lived in a big house. He had a beautiful garden, but he never let anyone enter it. Whenever he was away, some children from the neighbourhood would come into his garden to play.

One day, when the giant was not home, the children came to play as usual. When he returned, he saw the children playing happily in his garden. This made him very angry. He chased all the children away and then built a tall wall around the garden.

The children could not climb the wall to enter the giant's garden. Without happy children in the garden, all the flowers died. The leaves curled up and became dry. No new flowers, leaves or plants grew. In winter, snow fell and covered the whole garden.

When spring came, everywhere, trees grew new leaves and buds. Soon, there were green leaves and beautiful flowers everywhere. Birds sang on trees, bees buzzed around flowers and animals played around bushes.

But, it was still winter in the giant's garden. No leaves grew on trees. There were no flowers and no birds. The giant got worried. He wondered why winter did not leave his garden.

Then, one morning, the giant heard a cuckoo singing. Amazed, he went out to see the cuckoo. He saw a few children playing in his garden. Then, he noticed a tiny hole in his garden's high wall.

Think and Say

Tiny saplings have appeared in your garden. Your neighbour's ball falls on them and crushes them. What will you do?

The children had squeezed through it. When they happily played in the garden, winter left taking all the snow and cold with it. Spring happily entered the giant's garden. Trees bloomed with new leaves and flowers. Birds sang on every tree. He could even see small animals going happily about their business in the garden.

The giant realized that he had been wrong! He had been selfish. He had not shared his beautiful garden. He had not shared the joy his garden gave him with the children.

From that day onwards, he let the children play in his garden. Sometimes, when they were all having fun, the giant would sit and enjoy looking at them playing, too.

Remember

- Share your thoughts and feelings with your parents.
- Share your toys and games with your friends and cousins.
- Share your notes with your classmates.
- Take care of things that are shared with you.
- Remember, sharing is a good habit.

Figure out

Tick (✓) the correct answers.

1. The giant made a high wall around the garden because
   a. he did not want the children to play in his garden. ☐
   b. he loved the children. ☐

2. The giant had chased all the children away from his garden because
   a. he did not want to share his garden with anyone.
   b. it was very cold in his garden.

3. The giant realized that he had been selfish when
   a. spring came into his garden with the children.
   b. his friends told him so

4. When there were no children in the garden
   a. the garden bloomed in beautiful colours.
   b. the garden grew no new leaves or buds.

5. After realizing the value of sharing, the giant would
   a. share things with others.
   b. not share things with others.

B. Answer these questions orally.

1. Why did the children play in the giant's garden only when he was not at home?
2. Did spring come to the garden after the children had left?
3. Why was the giant amazed to hear a cuckoo in his garden?

Relate

Draw a 🙂 for the best answer.

1. Your father made pasta for you. You know that your friend loves pasta. What would you do?
   a. I would pack some pasta for my friend.
   b. I would eat the pasta all by myself.

2. Your cousin really likes the new shirt that you bought. He asks you if he could borrow it for a party. What would you do?

a. I would not lend the shirt.

b. I would lend the shirt happily to my cousin.

3. Your house help's daughter does not have toys or games to play with. When she sees you play, she becomes sad. How would you behave?

a. I would give her some of my toys and games to play with.

b. I would ask her not to be sad.

Workout

1. The words sharing, caring and giving have a lot of letters in common. Mix and match letters from each word and come up with new words.

SHARING	CARING	GIVING
....	....	....
....	....	....

2. Colour the picture and talk about it in class.

Let's carpool

Happiness Box

1. Read this poem aloud in class.

Box of Crayons

I had a box of crayons,
beautiful, bright and new!
I lent a friend a crayon,
But-oops-it broke into two!
My friend was sad and sorry,
But I said, 'I don't care,
'cause now we both can colour
with one crayon—we can share!'

2. How would you feel in the given situations? Choose any one of the emoticons.

angry happy afraid surprised sad

- You see a bigger piece of cake in your sister's plate
- Your mother is giving your favourite cookies to your cousins
- Your father is playing chess with your sister

Teaching tips

- Tell students to always speak the truth, whatever the situation.
- Stress on how students would feel if they needed something which their classmates or siblings refused to share.
- Encourage the students to get their favourite books for the book sharing day.

2. The Mule's Lesson

Discuss

Do you also fight like Ritu and Akanksha? Do you think fighting on the court is a good habit? Discuss in class.

Read along

A trader set forth on a journey with an ass and a mule. Both animals were well-laden with heavy loads. The ass carried his load easily, as long as he walked on the plains.

However, when he began to climb the steep mountain path, his load seemed heavier. He found it difficult to carry such a load. So he requested his companion, the mule, to take a small portion of his load. The mule, however, paid no attention to the ass's request.

Think and Say

You need to leave to meet your cousin, but your mother has not finished the household work yet. What would you do?

Shortly afterwards, the ass fell down dead under his burden. The trader could not find another animal in such a wild region. He placed the ass's load on the mule, over and above the mule's own load.

The mule groaned beneath this heavy burden. He said to himself, 'If only I had helped the ass a little in his need, I would not be bearing all the load now!'

Remember

- Always cooperate with people around you.
- Cooperating makes things easier for everyone.
- If you cooperate with others, they will cooperate with you.
- Work together and you will be successful.

Figure out

Tick (✓) the correct answers.

1. The mule could have helped the ass
   a. by sharing his load. ☐ b. by showing smartness. ☐
2. Did the mule cooperate with the ass?
   a. Yes ☐ b. No ☐
3. The ass would have been alive
   a. had the mule helped him a little. ☐
   b. had he sat down on the road and not moved. ☐
4. How did the mule become the loser?
   a. The mule became the loser as he had to bear the load of the ass too. ☐
   b. The mule became the loser as he lost his companion, the ass. ☐
5. What lesson did the mule learn?
   a. The mule learnt that he should never travel with the ass. ☐
   b. The mule learnt that if you cooperate with others, you help not only them but yourself, too. ☐

B. Answer these questions orally.

1. Was the mule a good team player?
2. Why did the ass want to share his load?
3. At the end, did the mule have to suffer too?

Relate

Draw a 🙂 for the best answer.

1. You and your friend have a badminton match. You know the whole school will be watching. What would you do?
   a. I would try to take all the shots by myself, so that it looks as if my efforts have won the match. ◯
   b. I would play my best and try to win as a team. After all, I win if my team wins. ◯

2. Your father is in a hurry for his dentist's appointment. You have asked him to make sandwiches for you. What would you do?
   a. I would help my father make the sandwiches. ◯
   b. I would stay away from the kitchen. ◯

3. Your little sister has taken a parrot as a pet. She has gone for her class and it's time to feed the parrot. What would you do?
   a. I would complain that I have to feed the parrot. ◯
   b. I would feed the parrot happily. ◯

4. One of your team members is not feeling well but you have to complete the project. What would you do?
   a. Make him or her work no matter what. ◯
   b. Let him take rest as he is not well. ◯

Workout

Find these five words related to cooperation in the word search.

T	E	A	M	G	J	D	V	F
T	G	E	I	R	F	F	V	R
G	R	J	K	L	G	T	B	I
T	O	L	E	R	A	N	C	E
V	U	H	H	H	O	R	C	N
G	P	T	F	F	U	G	D	D
T	H	H	E	L	P	G	V	S

team
help
friends
group
tolerance

Happiness Box

1. Draw or cut out pictures of teamwork and cooperation from old magazines. Make a collage of these and write a few lines about working together. Share the collage in class.
2. If you are the leader of a team, what qualities should you have? Unscramble the following words to find out.

Qualities of a Leader

- META PSITIR ....
- TOLERCANE ....
- DISCILIENP ....

Teaching tips

- Tell students how an activity can be done faster if everyone cooperates.
- Include an activity in class where if everyone cooperates and quickly completes the work assigned, they can get extra time for sports, library or any other activity which they enjoy.

3. Birbal Delivers Justice

Discuss

The shopkeeper is trying to cheat the lady. Have you witnessed anyone being unfair? Discuss in class.

Read along

The global goal, Peace, Justice and Strong Institutions, promotes peaceful societies and access to justice for everyone. It also promotes accountability of institutions that can provide us justice. Let's see how a poor farmer makes himself heard in a King's court to get justice.

16 PEACE, JUSTICE AND STRONG INSTITUTIONS

Once, a cunning man sold his well to a farmer. Next day, when the farmer went to draw water from that well, the cunning man said, 'I have sold you just the well, not the water. Therefore, you cannot draw water from this well'. The farmer was shocked to hear this.

The farmer felt so cheated that he appealed for justice in Emperor Akbar's court. He narrated the entire incident to the Emperor. He then asked the Emperor for justice.

The Emperor called Birbal and handed over the case to him. 'Birbal please listen to the story of this poor farmer and see that he gets justice'. Once Birbal had heard the farmer's story, he called the other man to the court as well.

Next day, both men presented themselves before the court. Birbal asked the seller, 'Why don't you let the farmer use the water from the well? After all, you have sold the well to the farmer'. The cunning man bowed low and replied, '*Huzoor*, I have sold only the well to the farmer, not the water. And so, he has no right to draw water from the well.

At this, Birbal smiled and said, 'Very well! Since you have sold the well to this farmer, you have no right to keep your water in the farmer's well. You must either pay rent to the farmer to keep your water in his well, or you take your water out of his well immediately. You must keep what belongs to you with yourself. Am I right?'

The cunning man realized that it was not possible for him to cheat the farmer anymore. He apologized to him for his trickery and withdrew his claim over the water of the well.

The entire court applauded Birbal for his intelligence.

Think and Say

How can we avoid behaving unfairly and disrespecting the rights of others?

Being Assertive and Confident

Effective Communication

Being assertive means to express your feelings and views firmly and confidently without insulting the other person. We should express ourselves both verbally and non-verbally, in ways that are appropriate to our cultures and situations. This means being able to express opinions and desires, and also needs and fears. It may mean being able to ask for advice and help in a time of need.

Remember

- Being just and fair requires bravery.
- You need to be just even if nobody is looking.
- At times, being just can be very difficult.
- If you are just with people, people will be just with you.

Figure out

A. Tick (✓) the correct answers.

1. When the farmer wanted to use the water from the well, the cunning man said
   a. nothing at all. ☐
   b. that he had sold only the well and not its water to the farmer. ☐

2. The farmer went to Emperor Akbar's court because
   a. he had faith in the justice of Emperor Akbar. ☐
   b. he did not have the power to fight the cunning man himself. ☐
3. Emperor Akbar asked Birbal to solve the poor farmer's problem because
   a. Birbal had nothing else to do. ☐
   b. Birbal was known to be intelligent. ☐
4. The cunning man apologized because
   a. he realized that it was no longer possible to cheat the poor farmer. ☐
   b. Birbal had asked him to. ☐
5. Birbal solved the poor farmer's problem using
   a. the qualities of intelligence and justice. ☐
   b. the quality of patience. ☐

B. Answer these questions orally.

1. In which Mughal Emperor's court was Birbal employed?
2. What was the dispute that Birbal had to solve?
3. What happened at the end of the story?

Relate

Draw a ☺ for the best answer.

1. Your friend is facing a problem. She wants you to help her solve it. What would you do?
   a. I would try to avoid my friend. ◯
   b. I would listen to her problem and then decide in a fair manner. ◯

2. When we are just to others
   a. we get just behaviour in return. ◯
   b. we always get injustice. ◯

3. Your friend helps you to complete your project. When the teacher asks you who helped you with the project, what would you say?
   a. I would say that I did the whole project by myself. ◯
   b. I would tell the teacher that a friend helped me with the project. ◯

Workout

Child rights were made by the world's leaders more than 20 years ago. Look at some child rights doodles. All these rights are granted to children under the age of 18 years. Write how you feel about them.

Right to be with family or with those who care

Right to healthcare

Right to life

Right to relax and play

Happiness Box

1. Scales of Justice

You need

- A wooden stand as shown in the picture
- Thread
- Two metallic or plastic bowls with three tiny holes

Steps

- Knot one end of the thread. Pass the thread through the hole in the metallic or plastic bowls. Repeat for all three holes.
- Gather all the three threads and tie the loose ends together.
- Hang the bowls from the arms of the wooden stand at equal height.
- Your model of the Scales of Justice is ready.

2. Make a charter of rights for your class. Look at the list below and choose the rights you think you have. Keep the charter in your class.

We all have the right

- to receive education. ☐
- to be provided with a safe classroom environment. ☐
- to be listened to and given the opportunity to express our opinions. ☐
- to good quality study resources. ☐
- to teachers and adults who are caring and fair. ☐
- to have fun and enjoy our time during playtimes. ☐
- to be friends with our classmates. ☐

Teaching tips

- Stress on striving to be just in all our decisions.
- Tell students that being just can mean many things, such as being just to oneself, to one's family, society and parents.
- Tell the students that being just even when nobody is looking is the truest form of honesty and justice.

4. The Humble Scholar

Discuss

Aseem is a well-known musician yet he is bowing and thanking his audience. Do you think he is humble? Discuss in class.

Read along

Ishwar Chandra Vidyasagar was a great Sanskrit scholar. His name is well known in the history of India for having worked selflessly to help women and the poor. He was a great man, but an extremely humble person.

Once, another Sanskrit pundit wanted Ishwar Chandra Vidyasagar to explain some Sanskrit language rules to him. Ishwar invited the pundit to Calcutta for a discussion. The pundit was proud of his knowledge, and getting an invitation from Ishwar Chandra made him even prouder. He dressed himself exquisitely and set off for Calcutta.

As promised, Ishwar Chandra was waiting at the railway station to receive him. In the meantime, the pundit looked around searching for Ishwar Chandra, who he believed would be dressed as grandly as himself. However, Ishwar Chandra always dressed very simply. The proud pundit mistook him for a coolie.

The pundit called the coolie and ordered him to carry his luggage. The pundit asked the coolie, 'Do you know where the famous Ishwar Chandra lives?'

Ishwar Chandra nodded, 'Yes.' He set off carrying the pundit's luggage to his own house.

On the way, the pundit kept blowing his own trumpet. Ishwar listened to him silently. Upon reaching home, he opened the door and invited the pundit inside courteously.

The pundit was surprised! He realized that the person he thought was a coolie was none other than the great Ishwar Chandra himself. He felt very ashamed of himself. He was shocked by Ishwar Chandra's simple home and habits. After staying with Ishwar Chandra for a couple of days, and learning from him, the pundit returned home a humble man.

Think and Say

You have won the annual school singing competition for the second consecutive year. How would you behave?

Remember

- Practice makes perfect.
- Never be too proud of what you have achieved. Always aim higher, and try to do better than you did the last time.
- If you are skilled at something, help others who are trying to work on the same skill. At the same time, try to learn something from them.

Figure out

A. Tick (✓) the correct answers.

1. The pundit could not recognize Ishwar Chandra because
   a. he was looking for a man dressed as grandly as himself. ☐
   b. Ishwar Chandra pretended to be a coolie. ☐
2. The pundit could not carry his own luggage because
   a. the pundit was not as strong as Ishwar Chandra. ☐
   b. the pundit was too proud to carry his luggage. ☐
3. The pundit felt ashamed of himself because
   a. he blew his own trumpet. ☐
   b. he had very little knowledge of the Sanskrit scriptures. ☐
4. The pundit learnt from Ishwar Chandra Vidyasagar to
   a. carry his own luggage. ☐
   b. be humble. ☐
5. The pundit was shocked to see Ishwar Chandra's simple home because
   a. he was expecting a grand home of a famous man. ☐
   b. he had never seen such a house before. ☐

B. Answer these questions orally.

1. Who was Ishwar Chandra Vidyasagar?
2. Why did Ishwar Chandra Vidyasagar invite the pundit to Kolkata?
3. Why was the pundit really proud and why did he dress himself up exquisitely?

Relate

Draw a for the best answer.

1. If you come across someone who sings his own praise, what would you do?
    a. I would start competing by praising my own work.
    b. I would calmly tell the person that every one has some good qualities.
2. If you score the highest in class, how would you feel?
    a. I would feel proud and look down on others.
    b. I would feel happy but not proud because next time someone else may score better than me.
3. You have spoken rudely to your mother. What should you do?
    a. I should apologize to her.
    b. I should be angry at her and wait for her to apologize.

3. You have spoken rudely to your mother. What should you do?
    a. I should apologize to her.
    b. I should be angry at her and wait for her to apologize.

4. Your mother has bought you an expensive gift. What would you do?
    a. Show off your gift and tell everyone how expensive it is.
    b. Use the gift humbly and not brag about it.

Workout

All of you have read the famous story of 'The Hare and the Tortoise'. Complete the story with the help of the pictures. You can also use the words in the help box.

race	tortoise	rest	hare	finish line	sleep	slow

Once there was a .... and a .... The hare was proud of his swiftness and laughed at the tortoise for his .... movements. One day, he challenged the tortoise for a .... In the beginning, the .... was far ahead. He looked back and saw the .... struggling behind. He thought that the tortoise would take a lot of time and decided to .... The hare went off to .... while the .... moved steadily ahead. He crossed the hare and slowly reached the .... The .... was still sleeping. When he woke up, the tortoise had already won the ....

This story proves that pride does not take you anywhere, while being humble and patient makes you a winner.

Happiness Box

1. **With the help of the given words, write a short story about humility. Give the characters suitable names. Also, give the story a title.**

   money power beautiful bright man woman road car simple complimented

2. **Solve these riddles.**

   RIDDLES

   a. No sooner spoken than broken. What is it?

   ....

   b. What has a neck but no head?

   ....

   c. What belongs to you but is used by others?

   ....

   d. Everyone has it and no one can lose it. What is it?

   ....

   e. What has a face and two hands, but no arms or legs?

   ....

Teaching tips

- Tell students that there is talent and skill in everyone. Take time to encourage students to find something they are good at, and to bring reticent students out of their shyness.
- Stress on how some of the world's best in any field are very humble people. Illustrate the example of people like Dr A. P. J Abdul Kalam.
- Tell students that pride comes before a fall, and that there is always room for improvement.

5. Braveheart

Discuss

Do you always do best in your class, even if it means not getting good marks at times? Discuss in class.

Read along

Shalu the TV news reporter was interviewing Om Prakash Yadav. Om Prakash Yadav had received the National Bravery Award in 2011 from the President of India. Here is an excerpt from the interview.

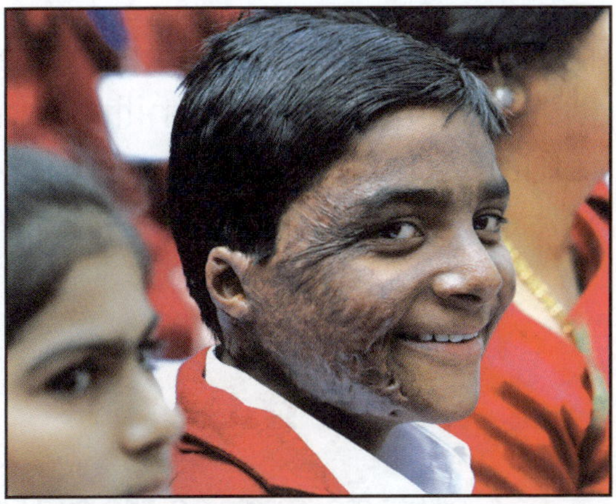

Shalu: Om Prakash, how old are you and where do you live?

Om Prakash: I am 14 years old and I live in Azamgarh in Uttar Pradesh.

Shalu: How far is your school?

Om Prakash: It is nearly 22 kilometres.

Shalu: That is far. How do you go to school?

Om Prakash: Eight children from my neighbourhood study there. So, all of us go to school in a van.

Shalu: Now, tell us what happened on 4 September 2010, when you were 10 years old.

Om Prakash: We had started for school in our school van. I was sitting near a the window. The van stopped to pick up two children. Suddenly, I saw flames in the gear box. The driver shouted, 'Get out! Get out!' He jumped off and ran into the fields.

Shalu: The driver ran away?

Om Prakash: Yes. The fire was spreading. I got up and opened the door of the van. The other children also stood up and started getting off, one by one. Six children got off safely, but two small girls were too afraid. They kept sitting. The fire had filled the front of the van. I quickly ran to the back and pulled out both the crying girls. By then, the fire had reached the door so I threw them out. My sleeve caught fire and the burning metal touched the side of my face. I jumped on the ground and dragged both girls down the slope before the van went up with a blast.

Shalu: That was a very brave thing to do! You could have saved yourself, but you went after those two girls.

Om Prakash: How could I leave them? They are like my sisters, and they were afraid.

Shalu: You are really very brave and certainly deserve the award.

Om Prakash: No, ma'am. I have not done anything special. I am sure, other children in my place would have done the same thing.

Shalu: My dear readers, Om Prakash is not only brave but humble too. Instead of being proud that he has been honoured by an award for his bravery, he believes he is like all ordinary children. It is this humility that actually makes him a special person.

Think and Say

Your friend wants to cross the road, but a dog is standing across the road. Your friend is very scared of dogs. What would you do?

Remember

- Courage comes from within.
- Stand up for something you believe in.
- Always speak up if you see some wrong happening.
- Help others whenever you can.

Figure out

A. Tick (✓) the correct answers.

1. Shalu the reporter was interviewing Om Prakash because
   a. he was a famous personality. ☐
   b. he had won the National Bravery Award. ☐
2. The driver of the van ran away because
   a. he had to get water to put out the fire in the burning van. ☐
   b. he was not brave. ☐
3. Om Prakash felt that he did not do anything special because
   a. he was a humble person. ☐
   b. anyone can save people from a fire. ☐
4. Did Om Prakash deserve the bravery award?
   a. Yes ☐ b. No ☐
5. If someone is afraid of something, can they still be brave?
   a. Yes, because bravery is about conquering fear. ☐
   b. No, if someone is afraid, they can never be brave. ☐

B. Answer these questions orally.

1. Why was Om Prakash given the National Bravery Award?
2. Do you think the two girls left behind in the burning van were not brave?
3. Do you think that Om Prakash is a humble person? Why or why not?

Relate

Draw a 🙂 for the best answer.

1. If you see your friends in trouble, will you help them out?
   a. No, I would not help them. If they are in trouble, they should get themselves out of it. ◯
   b. Yes, of course, I would help them. ◯
2. If you see someone doing something wrong, would you speak against it?
   a. Yes, I would speak up. ◯
   b. No, I would not speak up. ◯
3. If you see that a bookshelf is about to fall, what would you do?
   a. I would run away so that the bookshelf does not fall on me. ◯
   b. I would shout to make sure everyone moves away. ◯

Workout

On each step, write one synonym for brave. You can use the dictionary to find the answers.

COURAGEOUS

Happiness Box

1. Look at the picture and write how these people are brave.

2. Read the sentences and fill in the blanks with suitable words.

Sorry   Thank you   Please   Excuse me   Pardon me

a. ...., I forgot your book.

b. .... give me your notebook for a day.

c. ...., I could not follow what you said.

d. .... for this nice gift.

e. ...., I want to say something.

Teaching tips

- Stress on how simple actions can be acts of bravery.
- Tell students that conquering and overcoming fear are expressions of bravery.
- Ask the students to share examples of bravery from their daily lives.

6. Tina Goes Camping

Discuss

Have you ever planted a sapling or a seed? Discuss in class.

Let's work together,
And build a garden of our own.
It won't take much, it won't take long,
Seeds will bloom once they are sown.

Read along

Tina's class was going on a camping trip. She was very excited. She looked forward to spending a night under the beautiful stars.

Finally, after waiting for a whole week, the day for Tina's camping trip arrived. Her teacher, Roma Ma'am, took the entire class to a sanctuary nearby. Tina saw many fragrant flowers, tall trees, beautiful birds, swift squirrels and even a few deer, as they dashed through bushes and over green grass.

By the time evening fell, Tina had collected many fallen flowers, seeds and fruits. As she and her best friend, Anita, chatted about the day's events, they set up their sleeping bags. At night, Tina and Anita curled up inside their sleeping bags, warm and snug. They smelled the fragrant flowers, watched the glowing fireflies and heard the rustling of the leaves and the chirping of the grasshoppers. Happy and content, Tina, Anita, Roma Ma'am and the class soon fell asleep one by one.

When the class returned to school, the teacher asked them to make a project on the camping trip. They were to show this project after a few weeks.

Think and Say

You notice that a tap in your bathroom is dripping. What would you do?

For the project on the camping trip, Tina potted a plant from the seeds that she had collected on the trip. She also collected pictures of the things, seen during the trip, and made a collage.

By the time, it was time for her to show the project, her potted plant had grown pretty with greeen leaves and big red flowers. She showed the potted plant and the collage proudly to her class.

Tina was proud of her new green friend and vowed to respect nature.

Remember

- Plant more trees.
- Make people aware of the importance of trees and the need to care for them.
- Do not pluck flowers or leaves from trees.
- Water your plants every day and take care of them.
- Keep your garden and the park where you play, neat and clean.
- Use plant products like tissue paper, paper, paper plates, toothpicks and rubber very carefully. The more you use them, the more trees will have to be cut down.

Figure out

A. Tick (✓) the correct answers.

1. Which two animals did Tina see?

   a. Tina saw deer and squirrels. ☐

   b. Tina saw deer and lions. ☐

2. Who was Tina's new friend?
   a. Tina's new friend was Anita.
   b. Tina's new friend was a plant that she had potted.
3. What preparations did Tina make for the project on the camping trip?
   a. Tina made no preparations.
   b. Tina potted a plant and made a collage for the project on the camping trip.
4. What was Tina's collage made of?
   a. Tina's collage was made of pictures collected of the things she had seen during the trip.
   b. Tina's collage was made of random photographs.
5. Was Tina excited about sleeping under the stars?
   a. Yes, she was very excited about sleeping under the stars.
   b. No, it was just another day for her.

B. Answer these questions orally.

1. Who was Anita?
2. What was Tina looking forward to?
3. Make a list of the things that Tina saw during the camping trip.

Relate

Draw a  for the best answer.

1. There is a lot of leaf litter in your garden. What would you do?
   a. I would burn the leaf litter.
   b. I would collect the leaf litter in a pile and ask the gardener to use them for compost.

2. You notice that your friend wastes a lot of paper by making paper planes and paper boats. What would you do?
   a. I would tell him that he can use old newspapers to make paper planes and paper boats to save paper. ◯
   b. I would also start making paper planes and boats out of my own notebook sheets. ◯

3. Your younger sister wants you to pluck some flowers for her. What would you do?
   a. I would tell her that flowers look best on plants. ◯
   b. I would pluck some flowers for her. ◯

Workout

1. Festival of Trees

The festival of trees or *Vanamahotsava* is a day that reminds us all that we should take care of our priceless forests. Ask your teacher to tell you more about Vanamahotsava or learn about it from the Internet. Celebrate it in school.

2. My Camping Trip

Your family and you went for a camping trip to a nearby hill. Write a paragraph on all the animals you saw, the different plants you passed by and anything else that really attracted you. Try to include everything you can think of.

Happiness Box

1. Save trees by making your own recycled paper.

You need

- Old newspapers
- A big tub
- Water
- Wire mesh
- Two trays
- A rolling pin

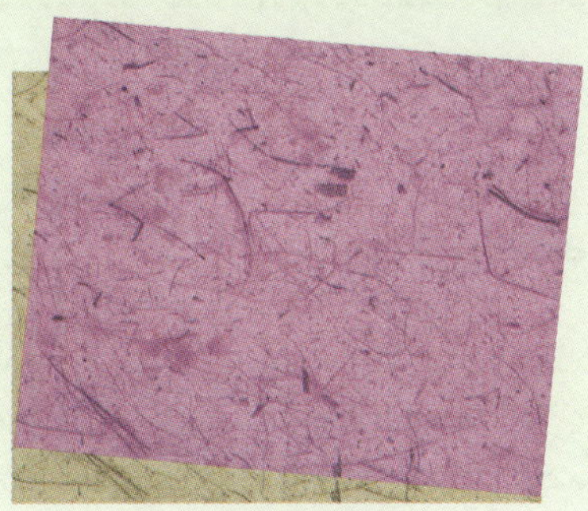

Steps

- Take old newspapers and tear them into small pieces.
- Soak them overnight in water.
- Blend the soaked paper in a blender to make a fine paste.
- Place the wire mesh in a tray.
- Spread the paper pulp in a very thin layer over a wire mesh. Wait for all the water to drain out.
- Gently remove the wire mesh from the tray and transfer the paper layer to a dry tray.
- Cover it with another sheet of paper and roll with the help of a rolling pin.
- Leave it to dry.
- After 2 to 3 days, when it dries, your handmade recycled paper will be ready.

You can also add husk, petals or leaves to make the paper beautiful. Colour can also be added to make different coloured paper. This paper can be used to make envelopes, greeting cards or even writing paper.

2. Complete these word associations.

a. Deforestation = Less trees; Afforestation = ...

b. More plants = Clean air; Less plants = ...

c. Water plants = Grow; Not watering plants = ...

d. Waste paper = More trees cut down; Saving paper = ...

Teaching tips

- Talk about the things nature gives us that we cannot see, like the air we breathe and utilities like natural gas.
- Talk about how plants clean the air.
- Stress on how different the world would be if things we take for granted went missing even for a day.

Happiness Activity

How do you start your day? Do you often rush to get on with your day. Try and start your day in a more mindful way.

Look at these activities. Try to do these in the morning and draw a 🙂 for activities that make you happy.

1. Lie in the bed and stretch ◯

2. Wake up, look outside and notice three things you like ◯

3. Hug your pet ◯

4. Step out, take a deep breath ◯

Practising mindfulness before going to sleep too can help us sleep better. We should:

- have a regular bedtime and wake up on time.
- keep our bedroom clean as cozy places help us sleep better.
- try to avoid playing games on gadgets before going to sleep.

Colour the poster. Circle the children who are showing bad manners.

A HUT
DONALD
BATA
LEE BOK
50%
OFF

Help Sahil meet his mother for lunch.

Project I : Dr A. P. J. Abdul Kalam

1. Read about the life of Dr A. P. J. Abdul Kalam from either your school library or the Internet. Now, answer these questions based on his life history.

a. Dr A. P. J. Abdul Kalam was born on ....

b. His full name is ....

c. His father's name was .... and his mother's name was ....

d. He was the .... child in the family.

e. He had .... brothers and .... sister.

f. At an early age, Dr A. P. J. Abdul Kalam sold .... to help his family.

2. Collect pictures of Dr A. P. J. Abdul Kalam from various stages of his life and make a collage in the space below.

7. The Bullock Cart

Discuss

Do you think life becomes easier when we work as a team? Discuss in class.

Collaboration

Read along

In a distant land lived a farmer and his wife. They had a bullock cart which they used to transport milk to the neighbouring villages. They were a happy couple and led a very contented life.

One morning, as usual, the farmer started his journey with large milk cans on his cart. As soon as the farmer was on his way, the wheels and the planks started talking. 'I was just wondering which is the most important part of the cart. Then, I realized that we are the most important part of this cart. If we don't move, the cart will stop!' said one wheel.

Hearing this, the planks got angry. 'Is that so? We think that we are more important than you. You see, it is because of us that you are attached. So, how can you be more important?' said one of the planks.

Meanwhile, the nails in the cart were listening to this conversation. As they were smaller in size than the other two, they felt neglected. So, the nails thought of teaching the wheels and the planks a lesson. 'The wheels and the planks think that they are the most important! Let us show them how important we are.' Saying this, the nails started twisting and pulling themselves out of the joints of the cart. Within a few moments, the wheels and the planks came off.

'Oh my God! Save me and my milk!' shouted the farmer as he fell down. All the milk spilled from the cans on the road. The poor farmer was almost in tears.

Seeing this, the wheels, the planks and the nails became ashamed of themselves. 'We should not have fought like this. Look at what we have done', said the wheels, sadly. 'Actually, each of us is important. It is because all of us are put together that a cart is made', added the planks. 'It is teamwork. None of us alone can make the cart move!' said the nails, agreeing with the wheels and the planks.

Though the milk was spilled that day, the wheels, the planks and the nails had learnt an important lesson. Never again was milk spilled because of silly discussions between the parts of the cart.

Think and Say

You see that two members of your football team have had a fight. What would you do?

Remember

- Teamwork promotes creativity, innovation and learning.
- Working together in a team builds trust among team members.
- We can learn to avoid conflicts or arguments by working as a team.
- Teamwork increases efficiency.
- Working together can reduce stress.

Figure out

A. Tick (✓) the correct answers.

1. The farmer and his wife lead
   a. a contented, unhappy life. ☐
   b. a contented, happy life. ☐

2. The wheels felt that they were the most important part of the cart because
   a. they thought that they were the ones who moved the cart. ☐
   b. they were very big in size. ☐

3. The nails felt neglected when the wheels said that they were the most important because
   a. they knew that they were very small in size and, therefore, not appreciated. ☐
   b. the nails were actually old and broken. ☐

4. The wheels, planks and the nails were ashamed of their behaviour because
   a. the farmer scolded them badly. ☐
   b. it was due to their fight that the farmer lost his earnings for that day. ☐

5. The message of the story is
   a. we should work together as a team. ☐
   b. a cart can be driven by wheels alone. ☐

B. Answer these questions orally.

1. Why was the cart an important possession for the farmer and his wife?
2. Why did the planks think that they were the most important?
3. Were the nails able to prove that they were the most important part of the cart?

Relate

Draw a ☺ for the best answer.

1. If you have to make a project, how would you prefer working on it?
   a. I would prefer working on it alone. ◯
   b. I would prefer the involvement and help of my classmates. ◯

2. What happens when you work in a team?
   a. The work finishes on time. ◯
   b. There is a lot of confusion and fights amongst team members. ◯

3. Which qualities can be instilled through teamwork?

   a. Patience, tolerance and appreciation ◯

   b. Superiority, pride and arrogance ◯

Workout

1. Make sentences with the given words.

Village ....

Realized ....

Twisting ....

Spilled ....

Ashamed ....

2. Some sports are very good examples of teamwork. Categorize the sports given in the box as solo sports, team sports or both.

archery	handball	badminton	squash	swimming
volleyball	boxing	water polo	cricket	golf
wrestling	football	lawn tennis	table tennis	athletics

Solo Sports	Team Sports	Both

Happiness Box

1. **Form groups of five and write a short story on teamwork. Draw pictures to go with it and share your story in the class.**

   Steps

   - Decide on a theme for the story. It could be an adventure, a horror or a fun story.
   - Decide the setting for the story. It may be based either in a village or a city.
   - Decide on the characters of the story.
   - Decide the plot of the story and how it proceeds.
   - Make a rough draft of the story. Then, edit and finalize it.
   - Draw pictures to illustrate your story.

   Ensure that all team members participate in storytelling.

2. **Complete the word ladder by making a new word with the last letter of the previous word. Use words related to team spirit.**

   C O O P E R A T I O N

   S U P P O R T

Teaching tips

- Discuss in class how teamwork simplifies the work at hand.
- Tell students how everyone in a team should be allowed to contribute as everyone is good at something.
- Stress on how a team wins only when everyone participates equally.

8. The Doves Unite

Discuss

**Do you help your classmates when they need your help?
Do you feel that you are a part of your class? Discuss in class.**

Winds blow the dust
but cannot move the rock,
United, the birds trapped in net
with the net, flew the flock.

United we stand, divided we fall
is a popular proverb,
Together in a bundle, sticks are unbreakable
but can break easily, if distributed to all.

So, if we are united
for the truth and the right cause,
There won't be any reasons
for our efforts to pause.

Read along

One day, a flock of doves found some rice grains scattered beneath a banyan tree. All the doves flew down to the tree and began pecking at the grains.

Suddenly, a net fell over them. They were trapped. They saw hunters carrying large bags coming towards them. The doves desperately fluttered their wings trying to wriggle out of the net, but it was no use.

The leader of the doves had an idea. He said, 'Let us all fly up together. Our united strength will help us carry the net off with us'.

The doves agreed to do as he said.

On the count of three, all the doves spread their wings and rose in the air. Their collective strength made the net rise with them. The hunters looked up in astonishment. They tried to chase the flying doves but could not. Carrying the net, the doves flew to a hill where the leader's friend, a mouse, lived with his family.

Think and Say

Your class is going to participate in a singing competition. You know that you are not a very good singer, but you want to be of help to your class. What would you do?

The mouse and his family used their sharp teeth to bite through the net. Slowly, large holes appeared in the net, and one by one, all the doves were free. The doves thanked the mouse and his family. They then, flew away together, united in their strength.

Remember

- There lies strength in unity.
- All of us together are stronger than just one of us.
- Ask for help when faced with a difficult situation.
- Accept help if you need it.
- It is all right to ask for help when you need it.

Figure out

A. Tick (✓) the correct answers.

1. The hunters were unable to catch the doves because
   a. the doves united and flew away. ☐
   b. the doves were flying faster than the hunters could run. ☐
2. Had there been only one dove, it would have been almost impossible to escape. Do you agree?
   a. Yes, I agree. ☐ b. No, I do not agree. ☐
3. Other than unity, what else helped the doves succeed in their plan?
   a. Their faith in their leader ☐
   b. Their struggle to free themselves ☐
4. Would the doves succeed if some of them had not helped the rest?
   a. Yes, they would succeed. ☐
   b. No, they would not succeed. ☐

5. Were the mouse and his family an important part of the team that helped the doves escape?
   a. Yes, they were.
   b. No, they were not.

B. Answer these questions orally.

1. Why did the net not rise when the doves fluttered their wings?
2. Why were the hunters astonished?
3. How did the mouse and his family help the doves?

Relate

Draw a 🙂 for the best answer.

1. The teacher has left the class for a few minutes. The class monitor asks everyone to do their work quietly. What would you do?
   a. I would do as the class monitor says.
   b. I would start talking to the other students.
2. You are the team leader of a project. You notice that one team member is not doing his or her share of work. What would you do?
   a. I would talk to the team member and try to resolve the issue.
   b. I would ask the team member to leave the team.
3. You see your friend is struggling to pick up something heavy. What would you do?
   a. I would let my friend struggle.
   b. I would help my friend.
4. You are on a hiking expedition and one of the hikers is injured. What would you do?
   a. I would continue to to hike
   b. I would stop and wait for the hiker to feel better

Workout

Look at the pictures. Write suitable sentences below each picture to make a story.

1. 

2. 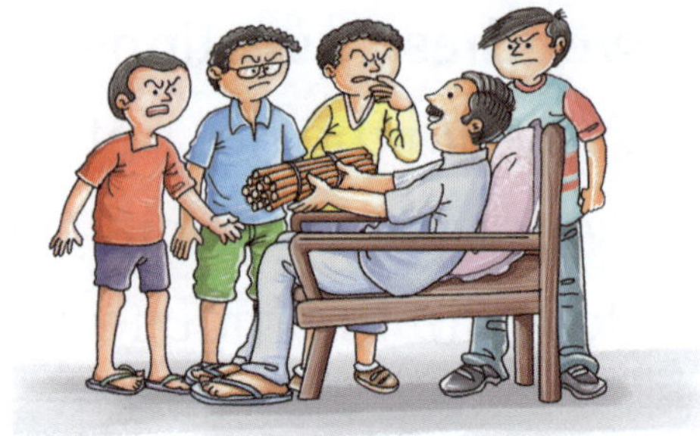

3. 

4. 

5. 

6. 

Happiness Box

1. Make a 'Unity Collage

You need

- A map of India
- Old magazines and newspaper
- Scissors
- Glue
- Chart paper
- Bold markers

Steps

a. Cut out the map of India and paste it on the chart paper.

b. Cut out pictures showing people wearing dresses of different states and paste around India.

c. Find a quotation on unity and write it.

d. Write the quote inside the map of India in an attractive manner.

e. Your unity chart is ready. Share it in class.

2. Unity in Community

If you look at the people in your community, you will see everyone looks different. Eyes, noses, skin color, even clothes make people unique. Everyone is beautiful in their own way.

Write two courteous phrases you will use with friends in your neighbourhood to make them feel a part of the community.

....

....

3. Complete the quotation.

United we stand, divided we ....

Teaching tips

- Stress on the fact that being united in doing something wrong is not ideal behaviour.
- Tell students that accepting help does not mean that one is weak.
- Tell students that helping someone when they need help is a good act.

9. Sid Wants a Robot

Discuss

Look at these pictures. Ahilya and Aamir behave in different ways. Why do you think they behave so? Discuss in class.

Read along

Siddhartha was waiting for his father to return home. He wanted to tell him about the 'Show and Tell Day' at school. When Father came home, Siddhartha started telling him everything.

'Dad', Siddhartha said excitedly, 'we had a 'Show and Tell Day' at school today. I took my favourite aeroplane to school. All the children had got their favourite toys. There were so many different toys. It was so much fun.'

Father smiled and asked Siddhartha, 'Well, that's nice! What else happened at school today?'

'Dad, Anurag got this really neat robot. It would do everything that Anurag said. Anurag asked it to sit, it sat; then Anurag asked it to bend and it bent. Wow Dad! It was amazing', said Siddhartha. He then continued, 'Dad, I want a robot like that, too'.

Father was surprised that Siddhartha had made such a demand. He said gently, 'Sid, Anurag's father works in a very big company. He earns a lot of money. Therefore, they can afford to buy expensive toys like the robot. On the other hand, I work in a small company and do not earn that much. Therefore, we cannot buy such expensive toys.'

'You always say this. We can never afford anything. I want that robot!' screamed Siddhartha and ran to his room crying.

That night both Father and Siddhartha were very upset. Grandmother saw everything, but she did not say anything.

The next day, in the morning, Grandmother served breakfast and called Siddhartha to the table. Once Siddhartha started eating, Grandmother kept serving him chapattis. 'I don't want more, Grandmother,' said Siddhartha.

'Aww Sid, you always say that! Take another chapatti, sweetheart,' insisted Grandmother.

Sid took another chapatti. When he had finished the chapatti, his Grandmother kept another chapatti in his plate. This irritated Siddhartha and he shouted, 'Grandmother, I have my limit! I cannot eat any more. Why are you forcing me to eat more than I can handle?'

Grandmother smiled and said, 'Exactly Sid! Just as you have your limits, your father also has his. When he said that the robot was beyond his limits, you should have understood.'

Siddhartha realized his mistake. He went up to his father, hugged him and said, 'I am sorry, Dad! I should have understood. I will not trouble you again.'

Father smiled and hugged Siddhartha.

Think and Say

You are in the market with your parents. You really like a toy there, but you have already purchased something else. What would you do?

Self Esteem

I am Special and Unique

Your self-esteem is how you feel about yourself. It is the feeling that you are a valuable person. We should never connect our self-esteem to things such as toys, clothes or the kind of house we live in. Our self-esteem comes from the love we receive from our friends and family. They alone can make us feel valuable.

Remember

- Thank your parents for whatever they have done for you.
- Donate the things you do not need. Don't throw them away.
- Explain to your younger siblings that everyone has a limit.
- Try to keep things like clothes, colours and bags in good condition so that your younger brother or sister can use them.

Figure out

A. Tick (✓) the correct answers.

1. Siddhartha was waiting for his father so that
   a. he could tell him about his day at school. ☐
   b. he could fight with his father. ☐
2. Father was surprised that
   a. Anurag had participated in the 'Show and Tell Day' at school. ☐
   b. Siddhartha had asked for an expensive robot. ☐
3. Siddhartha was angry because
   a. his father was refusing to buy him an expensive toy. ☐
   b. he had taken the aeroplane to school. ☐
4. Siddhartha was upset with his Grandmother because
   a. she was asking him to eat more than he could. ☐
   b. she was serving food to him. ☐
5. Siddhartha understood
   a. that everyone has their limits. ☐
   b. that everyone can afford everything. ☐

B. **Answer these questions orally.**

1. What did Siddhartha take to the 'Show and Tell Day' at school?
2. What toy did Siddhartha ask his father for?
3. Why did Grandmother continue feeding chapattis to Siddhartha?

Relate

Draw a 🙂 for the best answer.

1. You really like your cousin's expensive toy car. Before you play with it, what should you do?
   a. I should ask my cousin for his permission. ◯
   b. I should keep away the other toys. ◯

2. It's Diwali and you see some people who cannot afford to buy sweets when your vehicle stops at the red light. What would you do?
   a. I would pity them and move on. ◯
   b. I would offer them the sweets that I have. ◯

3. You go to your friend's house. You notice that she has a variety of chocolates. She offers you some. What would you do?
   a. I would take a few and thank her. ◯
   b. I would demand similar chocolates from my parents. ◯

Workout

1. **State whether true or false.**
   a. I always demand things from my parents. ....
   b. I ensure that I take whatever I like when I visit a shop with my parents. ....
   c. I throw the things that I do not need. ....

d. I always follow the rules set by my parents. ....

e. I shout at my parents when they do not get me what I want. ....

2. Find eight objects that you can buy by saving your pocket money in the word search. The pictures are your clues.

C	C	P	B	O	O	K	S	G	E
L	X	L	J	H	I	B	E	H	E
O	C	A	B	H	N	D	B	F	R
T	S	Y	J	B	D	K	E	W	G
H	E	S	F	N	H	N	L	F	S
E	H	T	H	B	W	A	T	C	H
S	N	A	V	D	D	D	D	K	O
H	B	T	R	B	A	G	F	H	E
T	B	I	H	H	T	B	G	T	S
R	C	O	L	O	U	R	S	R	F
G	Y	N	H	B	R	N	G	G	S

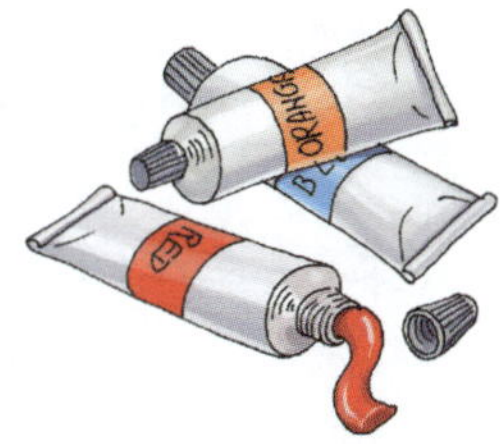

Happiness Box

1. Compliment Yourself

Self-awareness is the quality of being aware of one's own feelings or character.

Compliment yourself by ticking the sentences that are true for you.

a. I am strong. ☐

b. I am kind. ☐

c. I am smart.

d. I am brave.

e. I make others laugh.

f. I love to learn.

g. I love having fun.

h. I am great at science.

Write any of your good qualities that are not listed, here.

....

....

2. Make a list of things that you do not have but wish you could have. Make a plan by which you could save a part of your pocket money to buy an item from the list.

a. .... b. ....

c. .... d. ....

e. ....

3. Write thank you notes for the following people.

a. I thank my teacher for ....

b. I thank my grandmother for ....

c. I thank my friends for ....

d. I thank my neighbours for ....

e. I thank my father for ....

Teaching tips

- Tell students about good habits like saving.
- Tell students to focus on something that they want and to work for it. They should make a plan and share it with their parents. Whenever they are able to get the thing, they should show it to the class and talk about how they worked to get it.

10. Ekalavya

Discuss

Sam and Raghav are practising their game in order to perfect it. Do you also practise things that you need to perfect? Discuss in class.

Read along

Ekalavya was a small boy of the Nishadha tribes. He wanted to learn the art of using the bow and arrow. He asked Guru Dronacharya, the great teacher, to teach him. But, Guru Dronacharya refused to take Ekalavya as his student.

Ekalavya was not to be put off by this. He made a mud statue of Guru Dronacharya and placed it under a tree near his house. Every morning and evening, he would pray to the statue and put flowers before it. After that, he would start practising the art of using the bow and arrow. With regular practice, young Ekalavya was soon able to master the art.

One day, Ekalavya was practising, when a dog started barking. The barking disturbed Ekalavya. It started to bother him. When the barking went on for some time, Ekalavya shot seven arrows and filled up the dog's mouth without hurting it. With its mouth full of arrows, the dog could not bark any more.

Think and Say

You are finding a particular topic in Maths difficult. What would you do?

The dog ran away and entered Guru Dronacharya's ashram. When Guru Dronacharya and his students saw the dog, they were surprised. They wondered who could have done this. They searched the forest and found Ekalavya, who was silently practising his art. Guru Dronacharya was impressed. He said to his students, 'Look at this boy. He has learnt the art of using the bow and arrow through discipline and perseverance, even though he does not have a teacher. All of you should practise the same perseverance if you want to be good archers'.

Remember

- It is important to work constantly towards what you want to achieve.
- It might be difficult to keep working towards what you want, but you should constantly try doing it.
- You will be able to achieve what you want if you do not give up.

Figure out

A. Tick (✓) the correct answers.

1. Ekalavya was not put off by
   a. Guru Dronacharya's refusal to teach him. ☐
   b. the barking of the dog. ☐
2. Ekalavya made a mud statue of
   a. Guru Dronacharya. ☐ b. himself. ☐

3. Ekalavya was able to master the art of using the bow and arrow because of
   a. constant practice.
   b. the mud statue that he made.

4. Ekalavya did not hurt the dog. This showed that
   a. he did not want to hurt anything unnecessarily.
   b. he was trying to show off.

5. The story of Ekalavya shows that
   a. it is important to make a mud statue of your teacher.
   b. it is important to practise perseverance if you want to learn something.

B. Answer these questions orally.

1. Why did Ekalavya make a mud statue of Guru Dronacharya?
2. Why did Ekalavya shoot arrows at the dog?
3. What did Guru Dronacharya tell his students when he saw Eklavya's skill?

Relate

Draw a for the best answer.

1. Your cricket team has a match next week. You know that you need to practise your bowling. What would you do?
   a. I would take out time and practise my bowling.
   b. I would not practise as I know that either way we will win the match.

2. You have been learning how to dance, but you are unable to learn a particular step. What would you do?
   a. I would ask my teacher to change the step.

b. I would practise the dance step at every opportunity.

3. You know that your sister has been preparing very hard for her exams. Today, she is feeling sad and does not want to study. What would you do?
   a. I would support her and tell her it is all right to not study.
   b. I would ask her to take a break and then continue studying.

Workout

Split the following numbers into their place values. Draw the number of ice creams according to the number value. Let's see if you get all of these correct.

a. 59874 b. 21478 c. 23547 d. 456 e. 324

	Ten Thousand	Thousand	Hundred	Ten	One
a.					
b.					
c.					
d.					
e.					
f.					

Happiness Box

1. **Make this poster and keep it in your room.**

   Perseverance = If At First You Don't Succeed + Repeat

2. **I Don't Give Up**

   Draw a heart for the things you should do whenever you feel like giving up.

   - Try a different way to solve the problem. ☐
   - Ask a friend. ☐
   - Take deep breaths. ☐
   - Ask my teacher for help. ☐
   - Try again! ☐

3. **You want to go out for dinner, but your mother is watching her favourite show and has asked you to wait for an hour till the show finishes. List five things that you would do during this hour**

   a. ....

   b. ....

   c. ....

   d. ....

   e. ....

Teaching tips

- Make the students aware of the fact that success needs a lot of perseverance.
- Talk to them about the fact that continuous perseverance can become boring at times. In such a case, they can take a break and then come back to what they were doing.

11. Qutub Minar

Discuss

Do you recognize the pictures shown here. Have you visited these places? What is special about these places? Discuss in class.

Read along

The beauty of the city of Delhi lies in the fact that it was once the seat of many empires and sultanates. And so, the city is full of historical monuments. It has a strange blend of modern and ancient styles.

This was what Raj was reading on his laptop one day. He was reading about the monuments of India. Raj had browsed and read about the old, ancient buildings which stand even today. Raj felt proud of his country's national treasures.

Suddenly, his attention was caught by the picture of Qutub Minar. 'What a tall and royal tower this is! It is as if history is alive here. I wish I could go there and see it,' thought Raj. Within a few moments, the daydreamer in Raj was standing amidst the ruins of the Qutub Minar. He was surrounded by his classmates and the history teacher.

The gardens, the ruins and the minar—everything attracted him. Just as he was craning his neck to see the top of the minar, Alok said, 'It is hard to imagine that a minar that is so old can still be standing tall!'

'When was it made and by whom? Does anybody remember?' asked Miss Sharda, their History teacher.

'Yes Ma'am. I remember. It was made by Qutub-ud-din Aibak, the king of the Slave Dynasty, in 1192 CE', said Raj.
Miss Sharda smiled and said, 'Very good, Raj'.

Just then, they saw Nikhil writing his name on the wall of the minar with a chalk.

'What are you doing Nikhil?' cried Ananya, his friend. 'You can't destroy national property like this! This place belongs to our nation. Thousands of tourists from all over the world come every year to visit this monument. It is precious and must be taken care of. Such monuments are an important part of our culture, heritage and history'.

Nikhil was ashamed of himself.
He realized that he had made a mistake and stopped writing immediately.
Miss Sharda was happy. She said, 'Well done, Ananya! It is our responsibility to take care of our national monuments'.

They walked through the ruins and looked closely at the fine filigree work on the minar. A few bits of stones were hanging loose and Arijit tried to break off a little piece but his teacher stopped him right in time.

'This minar is already broken. What will happen if I break a piece and take it home as a memento?' he asked.

Miss Sharda told them that it belonged to all of us. Was it correct to break our own things?

The children discussed the minar and exchanged little bits of information. Raj came to know that the Qutub Minar had 379 stairs till the top, it is 72.5 m tall and that it is the tallest brick minaret in the world. But the most important thing he learnt was to respect national property and to feel proud of them.

Think and Say

Your classmate is scribbling something on the desk with a compass. What would you do?

Remember

- Historical monuments are our national heritage and should be respected.
- All national symbols are our national heritage.
- Be proud of your heritage.
- Talk to your younger sister or brother about your national heritage and how they should learn to respect it.

Figure out

A. Tick (✓) the correct answers.

1. What was Raj reading on his laptop?
   a. Raj was reading about the ancient monuments of India. ☐
   b. Raj was reading about the theatre groups of India. ☐
2. The picture of Qutub Minar caught Raj's attention as it
   a. was a 3D picture. ☐
   b. showed Qutub Minar as a tall and royal tower. ☐
3. Ananya stopped Nikhil from writing on the minar. Was she right in doing so?
   a. Yes, the minar is our national heritage and we should take care of it. ☐
   b. No, how does it matter where we write? ☐
4. How many stairs does the Qutub Minar have?
   a. 358 stairs ☐ b. 379 stairs ☐
5. What was the most important thing that Raj learnt from his trip to the Qutub Minar?
   a. Raj learnt to respect national properties and feel proud of heritage buildings. ☐
   b. Raj learnt that it was all right to spoil heritage buildings. ☐

B. Answer these questions orally.

1. Who was Nikhil? What was he doing?
2. Who scolded Arijit and why?
3. Write two interesting facts about the Qutub Minar.

Relate

Draw a ☺ for the best answer.

1. If you see some people writing or engraving their names on a historical monument, what would you do?
   a. I would ignore them and walk away. ◯
   b. I would ask them not to destroy our national property. ◯

2. There is a small monument near your house that, you have come to know, is historically important. What would you do?
   a. I would not do anything as there are many small monuments around my house. ◯
   b. I would write a letter to the Archaeological Survey of India asking them to take a look at the monument. ◯

3. Your class teacher is taking you to visit a national monument. What preparations would you make for the trip?
   a. I would read about the national monument we would be visiting. ◯
   b. I would not make any preparations for the trip. ◯

Workout

Find out the meanings of the given words from a dictionary. Also, make sentences from each.

Archaeology ....

Heritage ....

Ancient ....

Monument ....

Happiness Box

1. Make a project on the monuments of a city of your choice. Stick pictures and write short paragraphs on each.

You need

- Interleaf sheets
- Pictures of the monuments
- Cardboard folder
- Glue

Steps

- Choose of the monuments that you want to work on.
- Get their pictures and their details from the Internet.
- Stick the pictures on the blank side of the interleaf pages.
- Write the description for each of the monuments on the opposite page.
- Make a nice cover for the file.

2. Draw pictures of things that you feel represent India.

Teaching tips

- Stress on how tourists love our country.
- Talk about the history of some of the monuments in your area so that the students get interested in them.
- Tell students that each monument has a story and that they remind us today of what life was like yesterday.
- Organize a 'Heritage Walk' in your area.

12. Different Yet United

Discuss

India is known for its diversity. Discuss the different areas where you see diversity in India.

Read along

Ashish's birthday was approaching. Each year, his parents organized a party for his birthday which his friends really enjoyed. It was always great fun to attend Ashish's party.

This time, Ashish had a unique plan for his birthday party. He had friends from all corners of India. He knew that all of them looked different and came from different states. He wanted to organize a theme party based on different foods from these states of India.

He shared the idea with his parents. 'This time I want to have my birthday party based on the favourite foods of my friends. We will get the popular regional food of the states my friends belong to. Once they eat the food of their own state, they will love to taste and appreciate the food of other states too'.

'Wow! What a brilliant idea', exclaimed his mother.

His father agreed too. 'We will do just that, Ashish', he said.

So, preparations were made. Ashish made a list of the states his friends belonged to and their favourite dishes.

'Arha is from Assam, Abdul is from Himachal Pradesh, Lalitha is from Kerala, Ajeet is from Rajasthan and Abhay is from Gujarat,' said Ashish.

'So, which dishes do you want to get made for the party, Ashish?' asked his mother, a little worried.

'Mom, I think we will get *pitha* for Arha, *madra* for Abdul, *idlis* for Lalitha, *gatte ki sabzi* for Ajeet, and for Abhay, we will get *shrikhand,* which is a well-known sweet dish from Gujarat. I know that these are my friends' favourite dishes, too', suggested Ashish.

At last, the day of the party arrived. Ashish and his parents had all the arrangements made. Their house looked beautiful with all the decorations and smelt even better with all the different types of food. In the evening, when Ashish's friends started arriving, he became really excited.

The children sang, danced, played games and enjoyed themselves. After cutting the cake, Ashish took his friends to the dining table.

'Well friends, today I have arranged something special for you', saying this, Ashish uncovered the dishes one by one. His friends were surprised to see the different varieties of food presented on the table.

'That's *madra*' exclaimed Abdul happily.

'And is that *pitha*?' asked Arha.

'*Idlis*!' cried Lalitha happily.

Think and Say

Your favourite festival is approaching. Would you invite your friends from different states to take part in the festivities?

When the *gatte ki sabzi* and *ghevar* were uncovered, Ajeet and Abhay were also pleasantly surprised. The children loaded their plates and started discussing the different festivals and occasions when these dishes were made at their houses.

'We know that our country has so much diversity with different cultures, food and dresses. This party has made us aware of those differences and that we love being different. It gives us a chance to enjoy variety. Thanks Ashish, for this brilliant party', said Abdul excitedly.

The unique party was finally over. All the children were happy about tasting the food from the different states of India. Through this party, they also realized that Indians are united in spite of so many differences. The children also learned to respect and appreciate the food and customs followed in other parts of India. The children felt proud to be a part of such a diverse country!

Remember

- Respect and love not just your own state but the other states of India too.
- Try to learn about the culture and lifestyle of people from all states of India.
- Try to imbibe good things from the culture of other states.
- Enjoy the culture of other states as well as your own.

Figure out

A. Tick (✓) the correct answers.

1. Ashish had friends from all corners of India
   a. who had different backgrounds and cultures. ☐
   b. who didn't like each other. ☐
2. Arha, Abdul, Lalitha, Ajeet and Abhay were from
   a. Punjab, Manipur, Tamil Nadu, Uttar Pradesh and Haryana. ☐
   b. Assam, Himachal Pradesh, Kerala, Rajasthan and Gujarat. ☐
3. The idea behind the unique birthday party was
   a. to make Ashish's friends aware of India's diversity. ☐
   b. to have a lot of fun. ☐
4. Ashish planned to have food from
   a. a good restaurant. ☐
   b. five different states. ☐

5. How did everyone like Ashish's idea?
   a. No one liked Ashish's idea.
   b. Everyone loved Ashish's idea.

B. Answer these questions orally.

1. Were Ashish's parents also excited about the party?
2. What were the food items served at this unique party?
3. Did the children appreciate the food from the different states?

Relate

Draw a 🙂 for the best answer.

1. You go to your friend's house and his family cooks something special for you. What would you do?
   a. I would appreciate it.
   b. I would refuse to eat it

2. You have guests from another state of India at your house. What do you do?
   a. I would be unfriendly.
   b. I would appreciate the chance to learn about their culture.

3. If you like a custom or tradition of another state. What would you do?
   a. I would just say that I like it.
   b. I would try to incorporate it in my life too.

4. Your friend is wearing the traditional clothes of his state. What would you do?
   a. Make fun of his traditional clothes.
   b. Appreciate his effort to keep the tradition alive.

Workout

1. Find out and write how these words are said in any two regional languages of India.

1. Children ....
2. Difference ....
3. Unique ....
4. Party ....

Happiness Box

1. Read and learn the national anthem of India.

Jana-gana-mana -adhinayaka, jaya he,
Bharata-bhagya-vidhata.
Punjab-Sindh-Gujarat-Maratha,
Dravida-Utkala-Banga,
Vindhya-Himachala-Yamuna-Ganga
Uchchala-Jaladhi-taranga.
Tava shubha name jage,
Tava shubha asisa mage,
Gahe tava jaya gatha,
Jana-gana-mangala-dayaka jaya he
Bharata-bhagya-vidhata.
Jaya he, jaya he, jaya he,
Jaya jaya jaya, jaya he!

2. Join the people and things that are Indian with its map.

a. Chess

b. Taj Mahal

c. Maria Sharapova

k. Panda bear

d. Sikh groom

j. Yuan

e. Statue of Liberty

i. Kangaroo

h. Rock Garden

g. Nelson Mandela

f. Idli

Teaching tips

- Bring out the differences, for example, between food and dresses of different states.
- Talk about how Indians celebrate some festivals around the same time in different states known by different names. For example, Baisakhi in Punjab is also known as Pongal in Tamil Nadu. These festivals are celebrated for the same occasion like harvest or new year.

Goal 4: Quality Education

1 out of 5 children between the age of 6 to 17 years are not enrolled in school.

Millions of children lack basic mathematical and literacy skills.

There is not enough education due to lack of infrastructure like schools and colleges.

There are inadequate training programs to develop and train teachers in classrooms.

School education of boys is prioritised over that of girls, especially in poor and rural families.

TAKE A STAND!

- Donate your old books and stationary items to:
  - Your helper's children
  - Local library
  - Orphanage
  - NGOs working for children's education
- Teach poor kids in your community. You can start with teaching your maid's children

Project II : Unity in Diversity

Make a collage on the topic—Unity in Diversity. Talk about diversity of food, dress, geography, languages and tourist destinations.

You need

- Chart paper of any colour (of a thick variety)
- Pictures pertaining to the themes
- Sketch pens
- Glue

Note: Do not use scissors to cut the pictures. They should be torn by hand.

Steps

1. Tear the sides of the pictures by hand so that the borders are uneven.
2. Paste them on the chart paper in an overlapping manner.
3. Ensure that there is no white space between the pictures.